A STEP BY STEP BOOK ABOUT
COCKATIELS

ANMARIE BARRIE

Photography:
Dr. Gerald R. Allen; Dr. Herbert R. Axelrod; Michael Gilroy; E. Goldfinger; Manolo Guevara; Ray Hanson; Bruce D. Lavoy; W. Loeding; H. Reinhard; Nancy Richmond, San Diego Zoo; Julie Sturman; Risa Teitler; courtesy Vogelpark Walsrode; Wayne Wallace.
Humorous drawings by Andrew Prendimano.

Distributed in the UNITED STATES by T.F.H. Publications, Inc., 211 West Sylvania Avenue, Neptune City, NJ 07753; in CANADA to the Pet Trade by H & L Pet Supplies Inc., 27 Kingston Crescent, Kitchener, Ontario N2B 2T6; Rolf C. Hagen Ltd., 3225 Sartelon Street, Montreal 382 Quebec; in CANADA to the Book Trade by Macmillan of Canada (A Division of Canada Publishing Corporation), 164 Commander Boulevard, Agincourt, Ontario M1S 3C7; in ENGLAND by T.F.H. Publications Limited, 4 Kier Park, Ascot, Berkshire SL5 7DS; in AUSTRALIA AND THE SOUTH PACIFIC by T.F.H. (Australia) Pty. Ltd., Box 149, Brookvale 2100 N.S.W., Australia; in NEW ZEALAND by Ross Haines & Son, Ltd., 18 Monmouth Street, Grey Lynn, Auckland 2 New Zealand; in SINGAPORE AND MALAYSIA by MPH Distributors (S) Pte., Ltd., 601 Sims Drive, #03/07/21, Singapore 1438; in the PHILIPPINES by Bio-Research, 5 Lippay Street, San Lorenzo Village, Makati Rizal; in SOUTH AFRICA by Multipet Pty. Ltd., 30 Turners Avenue, Durban 4001. Published by T.F.H. Publications Inc. Manufactured in the United States of America by T.F.H. Publications, Inc.

CONTENTS

WHAT IS A COCKATIEL?

Of the approximately 340 species of parrots, half are found in Australia and the Pacific Islands, 140 in Central and South America and the Caribbean, and the remainder in Africa and southern Asia. Though mostly inhabitants of the tropics, some parrots, such as the Cockatiel, are also found in subtropical and temperate regions.

All parrots have hooked bills, feet with two toes facing forward and two facing backward, a comparatively large skull, and special feathers called "powder downs."

Cockatiels are the second most popular species of parrot after the Budgerigar, or parakeet. They can be found in Australia traveling in pairs or small flocks. Unlike most Australian parrots, which can be classified in one of three families, the Cacatuidae, Loriidae, or Psittacidae, the Cockatiel shares characteristics common to two families. Some taxonomists place them in the Psittacidae, but due to the erectile crest, male and female coloration, and nesting behavior, Cockatiels are considered part of the cockatoo family (Cacatuidae) by many other bird lovers. The scientific name of the Cockatiel is *Nymphicus hollandicus*.

In their native Australia, Cockatiels are known as quarrion. Being nomadic creatures, their movements follow the availability of food. Their diet consists of grains, fruits, berries, seedling grasses, other plants, and even cultivated crops.

Cockatiel nests are in the hollows of trees, sometimes

FACING PAGE:
Breeding in captivity has produced some delicately colored Cockatiel strains.

What is a Cockatiel?

The Lutino Cockatiel lacks dark pigmentation.

as high as six feet or more above the ground. They can be found near fresh water, such as rivers and creeks.

In the wild, Cockatiels are predominantly gray. As a result of domestication, it is common to see new color varieties being sold. Some of these are referred to as Pied, Pearl, Cinnamon, Lutino, and Silver.

Cockatiels average twelve inches in length from the beak to the tip of the tail. Their first molt is between six and nine months of age. Thereafter, they molt yearly, usually after breeding. They may live as long as twenty or twenty-five years.

FACING PAGE: This coloration is exhibited by male Cockatiels in the wild.

A mixture of light and dark colors in the plumage characterizes Pied Cockatiels.

COCKATIELS AS PETS

Cockatiels are well suited to life in captivity. Their low cost, small size, cleanliness, and hardiness make them ideal pets. In addition to their attractive appearance, Cockatiels are intelligent, alert, and inquisitive. They are friendly to people and other birds, and actually solicit attention. Some enjoy being picked up and stroked.

Extremely docile and long-lived, Cockatiels require ample space and a simple diet. Their ease of care, willingness to breed, and low cost make them a good pet for beginners acquainting themselves with the basics of birds.

Choosing a Cockatiel for a household pet has many advantages. Cockatiels require little time for training and maintenance and are easy to handle and relatively clean. They are readily adaptable to changes in their environment and are easily transported. Cockatiels pose no danger or harm to children or visitors. They can be kept safely out of the way, yet still provide an enjoyable source of entertainment. Since cockatiels require little supervision, they can be left alone for hours or even days at a time with sufficient food and water. They won't disturb your neighbors with lots of noise. They have a low initial purchase cost and the subsequent expenses are minimal. Disadvantages need to be considered when buying any pet. Cockatiels are susceptible to drafts and sensitive to an unbalanced diet. If you are planning an extended trip, a reliable friend must visit the bird every other day to replenish the food and water and clean the cage floor.

Your cockatiel will benefit from exercise. There are no accounts of a housebroken cockatiel. Droppings are likely to be found around the flying area. Also, furniture and other items may be chewed as the bird explores.

FACING PAGE: The author, Anmarie Barrie.

SELECTION

The first decision to be made is where to buy your Cockatiel. Choose a pet shop or bird store with a good inventory and clean, neat cages. Seek out well-informed employees for reliable, experienced advice in selecting a suitable bird and the proper equipment. I purchased my bird from a shop specializing in fishes and birds. The owner personally picks out each bird to be sold in his store from local breeders.

Having chosen the store, it is now time to choose your pet. The best times for selection are in the morning when the birds are first awake and early in the evening when they are active again.

Observe the Cockatiels' behavior as long as possible. To judge their activity, stand back from the cage so as to not interfere with their natural movements. Look for a bird that is bright, alert, and displays an active interest in its food. Note any prolonged motionless periods or signs of lethargy. A fluffed and tired look may mean the bird is sleepy, but it can also be a sign of illness!

Choose a Cockatiel with full, healthy plumage, which is essential for flight and insulation. Overall, it should look sleek, well groomed, and bright eyed. Avoid a bird with fluffed feathers or watery eyes and nostrils. Remember, the most important consideration is buying a healthy bird.

Examine the bird thoroughly in the store. Make sure it moves well. Handle the bird. The breast should be broad and feel firm, full, and plump. There should be no bare spots on its body. The bird should be clean and not soiled around the vent. It should have no sores or wounds. Be sure to take note of the

FACING PAGE: Pet shops usually have a selection of Cockatiel color varieties for sale.

droppings: they must be firm, not loose and watery, and the color should be a mixture of green and white.

Young cockatiels, around twelve weeks old, are easiest to tame. (If you don't want to tame the bird yourself, you may be lucky enough to find a shop that offers hand-tamed birds.) If you are choosing a bird for immediate breeding, though, an age of one and a half to two years is more desirable.

Similarities between youngsters and adults, and males and females, make it difficult to sex and age many of these birds. It is easiest to determine sex in the normal gray Cockatiels now that many color varieties are available. In some of these varieties sex determination cannot be made until after the first molt. Rely on your pet dealer for help in identifying a suitable bird. Keep in mind that the rarity of the variety, age, and tameness will affect the price. Discussed below are a few simple, though not foolproof, guidelines for assessing age and sex.

In some color varieties, plumage differences are sufficient to give a fairly reliable indication of sex.

Selection

This bird exhibits many of the characteristics of young Cockatiels.

Young birds are more slender than adults. Although they are about the same length, full size is not reached until around nine months, or after the first molt.

Adult feathers and beaks are darker overall. Young birds have pinkish or light gray bills that darken with age. They may also have "quills" on the top of their heads, undeveloped feathers behind the crest. This crest is more often erect in the young, but at least partially depressed in adults.

In gray Cockatiels, both male and female chicks resemble adult females. Yellow and gray barring is visible on the underside of the body and tail feathers, and yellow blotches on the primary wing feathers. At about six months, or after the first molt, the barring fades in adults, and males begin to exhibit a bright yellow head while their bodies become darker. So, if you see a bird with a bright yellow head, you can be sure it is at least six months old. The yellow marks on the wings and tail feathers also disappear. In the female, the yellow facial col-

oring merely outlines the features. The females are more drab, with the colors around the head more dull. In the white Cockatiel the sexes remain almost identical, although the females will likely be paler.

Spend some time listening to the birds in the store. Females are naturally quieter; therefore males are better to train to talk.

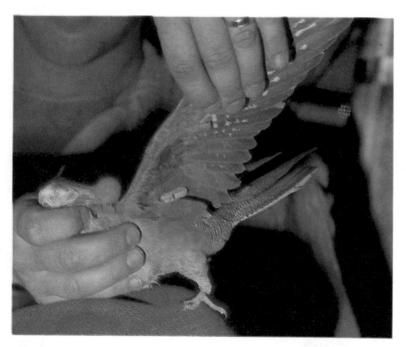

Barred markings on the undersides of the wing and tail feathers are found on some varieties of female Cockatiels.

If you want to tame the bird, keep in mind that a singly kept bird is more easily tamed and taught to talk. It is not necessary to buy two birds at once if companionship for the bird is a concern. Cockatiels are very adaptable to their surroundings and receptive to the attention of their owners and others. For taming purposes, birds should be kept separated anyway, because they will take too much interest in one another.

Selection

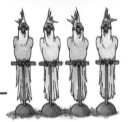

   When you bring the bird home, it will probably be placed in a box. Have everything at home prepared in advance for the arrival of your bird. This will lessen the time it has to spend in the box and minimize any disturbances from setting up.

   During transport, keep the bird warm. Do not move it on a damp, very cold, or windy day. It will experience enough shock in transit, so avoid any additional trauma as much as possible. This will also lessen the chances of the bird becoming ill.

   If it can be arranged, bring the bird home early in the day to allow it time to adjust. You will be able to spend some time with it before settling down for the night.

In many instances, a cardboard box is the best way to transport a Cockatiel.

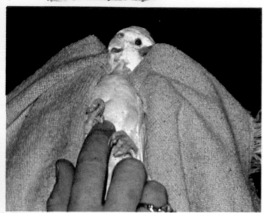

When the Cockatiel has been caught, take advantage of the opportunity to examine it for illness.

Be sure to re-examine the bird at home after it has had some time to settle down and recover from the stress of transport. If it seems ill, do not hesitate to call the seller. The longer the lapse of time, the less responsibility he will take. Do not be alarmed, though, if your bird remains motionless for prolonged periods. It may eat very little for the first few days.

An untrained bird may shiver when it is nervous or closely watched. This could be a sign of illness, but for your

Untame Cockatiels typically retreat to the upper corner of the cage when approached.

Selection

Catching Cockatiels must be done carefully, to prevent injury to the bird.

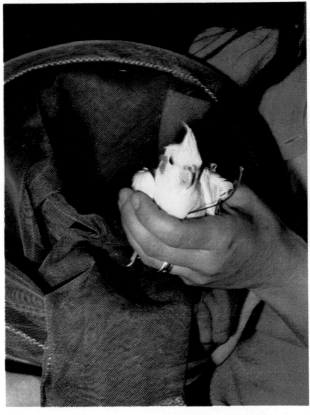

new arrival it is probably the result of unfamiliarity with close human contact.

If you lack experience in handling birds, you may be a bit timid. Just remember that the bird is more afraid of you than you are of it. Use a firm but gentle touch when taking the bird out of the box and putting it into the cage. Wearing thin cotton gloves will protect you from its bite, even though Cockatiel bites are rarely painful or serious. Do not grip it by the tail, or all you will have is a handful of feathers. If the bird does happen to escape, capture it in a net or with a light towel or cloth.

You may wish to have the bird examined by a vet before bringing it home. Make arrangements with the seller for exchanging the bird if the vet finds it is not healthy.

CAGES

Cockatiels are native to large open spaces, so choose a cage with plenty of room (a Budgie cage is too small). It is better to have more length than height in the cage, because this allows more freedom of movement for your bird. Living in a small cage could damage a bird's feathers and subsequently cause a deterioration in its health. If, for some reason, a small cage is necessary, allow the Cockatiel daily flights for exercise.

One of the most difficult tasks in owning a bird is taking it out and putting it back into the cage. The door of the cage should be large enough for you to remove the bird while it is on your hand without having to touch any part of the doorway. Some cages even have several doors of varying sizes. The cage I chose has a small door through which I can retrieve the bird. It also has a larger opening that the bird can fly through by itself after it has been tamed.

Because Cockatiels like to chew, a wooden cage is not desirable. The bird will gnaw its way out in a short time. Select a wire cage that has horizontal wires for added strength. Since Cockatiels like to climb up the sides of their cages, these horizontal wires offer further opportunity for exercise.

Some cages come with a sliding tray that allows you to clean the cage without working through the door. Cages may also feature a grid that keeps the bird out of its droppings. To simplify cleaning, line the cage floor with paper, and on top of that spread sand or gravel for increased absorbency. Replace the sand and paper every two or three days, or whenever the messiness makes you uncomfortable.

Cages usually come with seed and water containers, but plastic or ceramic dishes can be used as well. Place them

FACING PAGE:
Horizontal cage wiring caters to the Cockatiel's
inclination to climb.

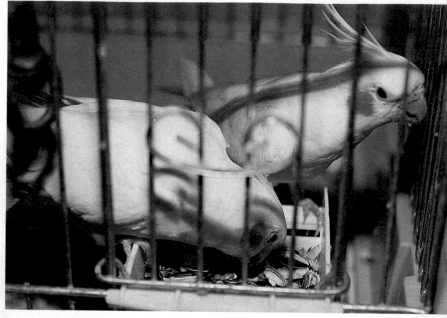

Most commercial cages have fittings to attach food and water cups to the wire.

on the floor of the cage away from any perches to prevent droppings from contaminating the contents. There are cages available that provide places for cups so they hang from the side of the cage. This avoids tipping and lessens the chance of droppings ending up in them. It is likely that this kind of cage will also have doors for each dish to facilitate cleaning and refilling.

To help decrease the scattering of seed, you might like to line the lower part of the cage with fine wire screening.

Wash and dry the bottom of the cage weekly and periodically wipe the cage bars. Scrubbing with a stiff brush will loosen dried debris. Clean the perches with a brush or sandpaper. Let them dry completely before placing them back in the cage. Wet perches can cause arthritis, rheumatism, and colds.

Do not clutter the cage with accessory items. If the cage does not come with a perch, select one or two of unfinished wood about ¾ inch in diameter. Toys, bells, or mirrors

Cages

can be hung in the cage for amusement. A branch from a tree that can be chewed and splintered is great fun. Be creative.

Once your bird is tame, you may want to provide more activities outside of the cage. A playground of ladders, perches, and toys can be fun for you and the bird. Be sure that all materials are nonpoisonous, unbreakable, and have no sharp edges.

Determining where in your home to place the cage is very important to the well-being of your pet. Select a pleasant

In choosing a location for the cage, the Cockatiel's safety is the most important consideration.

and comfortable room. Avoid kitchens, where sudden changes in temperature are frequent. The daytime temperature should average between 65 and 80°F. Nighttime temperatures can drop as low as the upper 40s.

Place the cage in an area that is well ventilated and free from smoke but away from drafty windows and doors. Captive birds have a thinner coat of down and so are more susceptible to chills. Avoid heaters and radiators that can be drying and thereby harmful to feathers.

Food and water vessels should be installed in the cage in locations where they won't be soiled by droppings.

Rest the cage on a firm and steady support so it is at eye level or higher. This may give the bird a stronger feeling of security. Be sure the cage is not exposed to direct sunlight for long periods; an area with indirect natural light is best.

At night, the room should be quiet and dark. If this is not possible, a drape or cloth placed over the cage will do as well. This cloth can also serve to quiet the bird should it become noisy or anxious. Keep it covered until it has calmed down, then remove the drape. Do not keep it covered once the

Cages

bird has quieted; it may just have been trying to get your attention.

If you would like to take your bird outside in its cage, hang the cage from a tree out of direct sunlight and away from potential predators. It is safe to have the cage on the ground only if the area is free from danger and under constant supervision. Your bird is a helpless victim. It can not flee from any threat that may present itself.

To be effective, the cloth used to cover the cage must be heavy enough to darken the interior.

Commercial Budgie (parakeet) mix, supplemented with a daily feeding of fresh greens, will provide the basic nutrients. Unsalted sunflower seeds, millets, wheat, oats, and safflower seeds may be added to the diet. This allows the bird the opportunity to eat seeds that may satisfy dietary needs. Your bird's digestive system will extract almost every nutrient available in the seeds.

FEEDING

Chicory, dandelion leaves, weeds, seedling grasses, carrot tops, watercress, spinach, celery, and peas are some of the greens that are good for your bird. Iceberg lettuce is of little value, so just avoid it. You can offer your bird a variety of fruits, such as apples, oranges, bananas, or whatever else it might like. Fresh branches from trees and bushes (oak, maple, or fruit trees, for example) also provide variety. Be sure vegetation has not been sprayed with insecticides, and always check food to be certain it has been washed clean. It may take some time for your bird to accept new foods. Always make them available so your bird can pick and choose for itself. Soon you will be able to identify your bird's own tastes. Never offer table scraps, which can result in digestive disorders.

You may even want to sprout your own seedling grasses from seed. At any rate, this is a valuable test for judging whether the seed is nutritious. If it does not sprout, then it is not good bird food.

A properly cared-for bird is likely to remain healthy. A poor diet may lead to illness. After your bird has calmed down and settled into its new home, be aware of how much and what kinds of food your bird consumes. Measure its food intake over

FACING PAGE: Besides nutrition, cuttlebone satisfies the need to gnaw and thereby helps to prevent beak overgrowth.

a period of time, at least a week. In the future, you will be able to note any changes that might indicate illness. During molting and in cold weather, your bird may eat more to produce more heat for warmth.

No more than a three- to four-week supply of seed should be stored, to avert spoilage. Seal it in moisture-proof containers and keep it in the refrigerator or some cool, dry place. Moisture and humidity can create mildew, which will make your bird ill. Also, in time, seed can dry out and lose its nutritive value.

If you follow this regimen, there will be no need for special foods, tonics, or conditioners. However, you may choose to add a soluble vitamin and mineral mixture to the drinking water.

Grit and Cuttlebone

Grit contains essential minerals and trace elements for your pet. It is stored in the gizzard as an aid in digestion, espe-

Treat foods, though nutritious, are not designed to be a staple part of the diet.

Feeding

cially of seed. The grit may contain charcoal and, preferably, some other organic material, such as oyster shell. If it does not, it can be bought separately and added to the grit. The organic compounds are especially important during breeding. Keep the grit mixture in a dish separate from food and change it about every week.

Preening, or grooming the plumage with the beak, serves to keep the feather vanes intact.

Cuttlebone is the internal shell of the cuttlefish, a marine animal closely related to the squid. It provides calcium for bones and feathers, strong eggshells during breeding, and prevents egg binding. During breeding, its consumption may be doubled or even tripled. Gnawing on the cuttlebone or a mineral block also keeps the beak from overgrowing.

Cuttlebone typically comes with a clip. If it has none, simply make holes in it and attach it with wire to the side of the cage near a perch.

Bathing

In the wild, Cockatiels are bathed by rain showers. You may find your bird likes to bathe, particularly in hot weather. Some pet birds, though, dislike water. Provide a bath for your bird, but do not force it to bathe. Your bird will use a gland at the base of its tail to get oil for grooming.

Fill a shallow (but heavy enough to avoid tipping) dish with water. Place it in the cage every few days for thirty minutes or so. If the cage is large enough, you can keep the dish in

Outdoors, a Cockatiel spreads its wings to dry after a bath.

it permanently. Just be sure to change the water every day because the bird may also use it for drinking.

You may prefer to allow the bird to bathe outside of the cage, especially if there is insufficient space. A bath dish can still be used, or you may let the bird use a sink. Some trained birds will actually fly to the sink when they hear the water running. The temperature of the water should not be very warm or very cool. You can give the bird a few light squirts

Indoors, a shallow dish can be provided for bathing.

with a sprayer, making sure not to soak it. If you observe a bird bathing in a dish, you will see that it will mostly wet its feet and belly feathers.

When you take the bird outside in its cage on hot days, you can gently spray it with water from the hose. Again, make sure the water is the right temperature and that the bird will not suffer a chill.

After bathing, your pet will preen and groom to reposition its feathers.

Preening between individuals often functions as part of courtship.

TRAINING

Cockatiels need to exercise their wing muscles. Fortunately, cockatiels are one of the most easily tamed caged birds. You may want to begin as soon as you bring the bird home. It may not be necessary to give the bird time to adjust to its new surroundings. Or you may want to allow your bird some time to adjust. Try to bring the bird home early in the day so it has plenty of time to settle down before dark. This gives it a chance to get accustomed to strange noises and activity. You may try to offer it some food and scratch its head. Use your own judgment; each bird has its own temperament.

At first, the bird may shiver or avoid your advances. Be patient. I kept my bird in the cage for a few days, periodically talking to it and moving close to the cage. Eventually, I put my hand inside and tried to touch the bird. Later that same day, I had the bird resting on my hand. From there I advanced to taming outside of the cage.

Young birds, around twelve to fourteen weeks, are especially easy to train. Older birds are seldom as friendly and are more quickly frightened. They require more time and patience. As with any bird, though, the more time invested, the faster the results. Have a family member with plenty of time and motivation do the initial taming. Give short lessons often. Give a taming lesson each time the bird is removed from the cage. The more accustomed a bird is to human handling the easier it will be to train.

Most importantly, the bird's wings need to be clipped. This will not detract from its appearance and is painless. Clipping is a helpful aid in training, and the feathers will regenerate in six months. If for some reason you never want to clip the wings, the flight feathers can be taped in a resting position during the first few taming sessions.

FACING PAGE: A hand-tame Pearl Cockatiel.

One style of feather clipping involves cutting the flight feathers just beyond the covert feathers.

Feather Clipping

Clipping your new pet's wing feathers will make taming easier. Taming can still be done without clipping, but it will be considerably more tiring. Also, when a clipped bird is let out, there is no possibility of its escaping. No matter how tame a bird is, it should never be taken outdoors without being clipped. Clipping the wings means that the bird will have its ability to fly limited. It will be able to travel only a few feet before landing.

If done properly, feather clipping is quick, easy, and painless for your bird. It can be done by one person, but it is easier with two: one holds the bird while the other clips. Of course, the clipping can be done in the pet shop if you prefer not to attempt it yourself. This will also prevent the bird from

associating a bad experience with its new surroundings.

Be aware that the flight feathers will be fully regrown in about six months. If you intend to keep your bird clipped, check for new growth periodically.

The feathers of one or both wings can be cut. It is best to clip only one wing, because then the bird will lose control over the direction of its flight. This will facilitate taming.

There are two methods of wing clipping: (1) cutting all the primary feathers, or (2) cutting some secondary and all primary feathers except the outer two or three. The second method preserves the long, graceful appearance of the flight feathers. Leave the outermost two feathers intact and cut the next two in half. Then clip the next eight to ten feathers at the point where they emerge from beneath the feathers that overlap them. Support the body of the bird on your lap or a counter. Never hold it by the neck or tail. If necesary, restrain its beak

Many people think that leaving the outermost flight feathers uncut maintains the appearance better when the wings are folded.

with your thumb and forefinger. Keep the neck straight without pushing or pulling its head. Use the other hand to hold the feet and torso. Hold the bird gently yet firmly, always monitoring respiration. Now extend the wing from the bend to get a clear view. Push up the under-coverts to expose the feather shafts.

Holding the scissors parallel to the leading edge of the wing, start midwing and cut outwards towards the primary feathers. Leave at least ½ of an inch emerging from the wing

Sharp scissors are sufficient to clip Cockatiel feathers. The task is made easier if another person helps by restraining the bird.

as the bases of the feathers contain blood vessels. If bleeding does occur, it will stop soon because cockatiels have good coagulating properties. Having styptic powder on hand is a good idea.

Working With the Bird

Have one person train one bird at a time. That same person should continue giving the lessons because having one trainer is less confusing for the bird. Only that person should be in the room during taming. The less activity there is, the less

Training

A Cockatiel bite, which may be painful, is done defensively, out of fear.

distraction for the bird. Also, choose a small, quiet room, one with little furniture and no high perches. Make sure there is no escape from the room through a window or door. Close the drapes so the bird won't fly into a window, and cover all mirrors. Have a stand ready outside of the cage to place the bird on after a taming session.

Speak and whistle softly to the bird to keep it calm. Grasp it gently and firmly around the wings. A nasty disposition may be indicated by hissing or biting. If it bites, do not make jerking movements which may be frightening. The bites are not severe and rarely harmful. If the bird does bite and continues to gnaw, put your thumb under its chin to make it release its hold. *Never* hit it; just say "No" loudly. The bird will soon stop. As a precaution, you can wrap your fingertips with tape or adhesive bandages for protection. A pair of thin cotton gloves can also be used. Don't wear bulky gloves. They make it more difficult to handle the bird and may be frightening to it.

If your bird is a biter, you may want to stick-tame it first. Then if it bites, the bird will grab and gnaw the stick. The bird may even respond better to a stick for moving it in and out of the cage. Once the bird is stick-tamed, the method can be used as a handy trick for removing it from high places.

Work with the bird close to the floor by getting on your knees. This avoids long falls. Release the bird repeatedly from about one foot off the floor. It will scamper on the floor, soon realizing that it cannot fly well.

Never alarm the bird, but be determined and persis-

tent. Move quietly and slowly. Do not sneak up on the bird and grab it from behind. A frightened bird is not trainable. Approach it from the front. It will realize no harm is intended.

Surround the bird from below with out-stretched fingers. Backing it into a corner may make this easier. Now coax it onto your hand. Let it perch until relaxed. Slowly lift your hand from the floor and stand up. This may need to be repeated several times before the bird will remain on your hand. Stroke the bird to simulate preening. Now it is a matter of getting the bird used to human contact. Some birds will not like the stroking; do not persist.

Offer a finger perch higher than the other hand. Press the side of your finger into the bird's breast region to throw it off balance and have it climb onto your finger. The bird may use its beak to steady itself, but this is not intended as a bite.

Once the bird will remain on your hand, you can coax it to your shoulder. With a rolling motion of your hand, the bird will be forced to step onto your shoulder to regain balance. You may even want it to try your head. Just remember, there is no such thing as a housebroken bird!

Handle the bird for longer sessions each day. It will react quickly to attention. If you allow the bird to come out of its

Training a Cockatiel is most successful when carried out in small increments.

cage to exercise, it will be in better health and friendlier towards people. To avoid a one-man bird, introduce other family members once the bird is tame. Have them feed and play with it.

During training, food may be a useful tool. Ration your pet's food and offer it as a reward for desired behavior. After a session, be sure to provide food and water, no matter the result of that session. Your bird will most likely be hot and tired. Now

Confronted by a perch at breast level, the Cockatiel is inclined to step onto it.

is a good time to place it on the perch outside of the cage and let it rest. If it flies off, simply return the bird to the perch.

The least you should expect from your pet is to have it rest comfortably on your hand. The test is to hold it gently cupped in both hands until it is quiet. If the bird wants to fly away, grip it again. Repeat this until the bird makes no attempt to bite or escape. With the bird feeling safe and secure in your

hands, it will be easier to examine and treat it in the future.

If you allow your bird to fly around your home, do not leave anything around worth saving that can be chewed. Provide plenty of toys for distraction.

In advanced training, your pet can be taught some simple tricks, such as climbing ladders and ringing bells. Natural behavior, such as spreading its wings on command, can be reinforced. Simply reward desired behavior with food and ignore anything else. Teach one trick at a time during short but frequent lessons, the same as in initial taming. Do not try to teach your bird difficult tricks; for these a larger parrot is required.

Once a Cockatiel has lost its fear of people, it may allow its feathers to be touched.

Talking

Cockatiels do have some verbal abilities. They can learn to repeat words and phrases and even whistle tunes. The length of time it will take is unpredictable, nor is talking guaranteed. After learning the first word, though, it will likely become easier, and your pet will continue to learn over the years.

Males are said to be superior in learning to speak; females are by nature quieter. A rested and relaxed bird will respond more readily and will probably better imitate someone to

Training

whom it is attached. Birds seem to respond better to the high-pitched voices of women and children.

Repetition, patience, and time are necessary in training. One bird at a time will be easier, because two or more birds will be interested in the others.

Developing a uniform schedule of daily training will likely facilitate learning. A half hour is sufficient, even if it is when you are cleaning the cage.

Choose simple words or phrases. Do not speak too quickly, and be sure the pronunciation is clear. Introduce one word or phrase at a time, and when your pet says it, keep repeating it until it is clear. The bird must be fluent before advancing. So, after a few days, begin with a new sound.

Training records are available, or you can make your own tapes to speed training. Treats are not necessary, unless you want the bird to speak on command. Then reward it for the desired speech.

Most tricks take advantage of natural behaviors—climbing, for instance.

DISEASES & FIRST AID

Cockatiels are remarkably free from disease. One reason is that their food in captivity is not too different from that in the wild. Of course, accidents and illness can happen, but do not panic. Refer the problem to your veterinarian. The birds are very hardy and with the right conditions will continue to thrive in captivity. Preventive maintenance is the most important aspect. Provide a clean cage and a balanced diet. With the proper care, an illness will be unlikely.

A lack of activity and ruffled feathers (in an attempt to preserve body heat) are signs of disease. Ill birds have difficulty maintaining body heat and experience a noticeable absence of appetite. Do not wait long to call your vet; weight loss can be rapid and fatal.

Isolate sick birds in a hospital cage. You can buy, rent, or make one yourself. Cover all but the front of the regular cage (or a smaller cage) with plastic or cloth to prevent drafts and block any outside stimulation that may excite your bird. A light bulb suspended in the cage or a heating pad placed in it will provide additional warmth. A constant temperature of 70 degrees is recommended.

Remove all perches and place the food and water containers on the floor. Your pet may become picky about what it chooses to eat, so supply its favorite foods. It is very important that it eat something, even though a balanced diet is still preferable.

Never give the bird any medications meant for human consumption, but adding to the water a general antibiotic from

FACING PAGE: Illness is more easily prevented than treated, and this is best accomplished by a careful attention to the Cockatiel's needs—as in providing a chew toy.

a pet shop or vet may facilitate recovery.

If it is necessary to transport the bird to a vet, keep it warm and quiet. Avoid sudden temperature changes.

Broken Legs and Wings

It is best to take your bird to the vet. Broken legs require proper splinting and bandaging to promote healing. If done incorrectly, the bird may be permanently crippled and unable to breed.

Wings are easier to set. Place the wing in a normal resting position and put gauze between the wing and the body. Bind with adhesive tape. Call the vet first. He may suggest leaving the injuries alone while healing. The bird will naturally favor the injury.

Remove the perches from the cage and place dishes on the floor to restrict movement. It will take about two weeks for healing. Disturb the bird as little as possible.

Lively behavior and alert, clear eyes are signs of a healthy Cockatiel.

Left untreated, respiratory infections like a cold can lead to severe, irreparable conditions.

Colds

Symptoms of a cold are similar to other ailments: lethargy and ruffled feathers, possibly accompanied by sneezing, coughing or wheezing. The bird may exhibit a nasal discharge and have sore looking eyes. Set up a hospital cage and add antibiotics to the water. If the condition persists, call the vet. When not properly treated, the cold can develop into pneumonia, asthma, and other chronic infections that are difficult to treat and possibly fatal.

Conjunctivitis

Your bird will shut its eyes often and blink a lot. The eyes will be watery. Apply chloramphenicol ointment for several days at four-hour intervals. This can be purchased at a pharmacy, pet shop, or veterinarian's office.

Constipation

There will be a lack of green in the droppings, or maybe a lack of droppings entirely. This is usually the result of an inferior diet. Feed the bird a tiny dose of milk of magnesia from an eye dropper or add 2-3 drops of lime water to the drinking water and correct the diet immediately.

Diarrhea

A more common occurrence, diarrhea is often the sign of another ailment. It is also the result of an improper diet or the consumption of unclean food or water. Add an antibiotic to the water and some vitamin B_{12} until the discharge is normal.

Cuts and Open Wounds

The bleeding will stop quickly if the damage is not too severe. Styptic powder will stop bleeding from small cuts. Wash the area with hydrogen peroxide and rub with an antibiotic salve. If the injury is more critical, consult a vet.

Feather Picking

A rare problem, feather picking results from an inadequate diet, usually one lacking in mineral content. Adjust the diet accordingly. Occasionally it is a sign of anxiety or boredom. Give your bird lots of toys and attention.

Psittacosis

This is a respiratory disease, rare among caged pets. It is a bacterium with symptoms similar to pneumonia. Imported birds are quarantined to insure freedom from this and other diseases because it can be transmitted to humans. A sound practice is to always deal with an experienced breeder or pet shop whose concern is to sell only healthy specimens. Definitely see a vet.

Going Light

The bird exhibits a marked loss of weight. Sometimes this is associated with another illness, sometimes the cause is unknown. Give an antibiotic in the drinking water and provide more fattening foods, such as oats, sunflower seeds, milk-soaked wheat bread and corn kernels. Your vet may also recommend an appetite stimulant.

Heat Stroke

Typically this is the result of a careless person who left the bird outside a long time in direct or reflected sunlight. Chances of recovery are slim if the time was very long, but if

Diseases & First Aid

detected soon enough, spray the bird with cool water or rub with a moist cloth or sponge.

Indigestion

Vomiting is a sign of infection or a poor diet. Give an antibiotic in the drinking water or change the diet.

Frequent cage cleaning is an important part of hygiene and disease prevention.

Mites

If you notice your bird scratching a lot, closely examine it and the perches. Remove the bird from the infested cage and disinfect cage and perches by using commercial preparations available in pet shops. These come in both spray and liquid forms.

Scrub the cage and perches with a stuff brush and do not return your pet to its cage until the latter is pefectly dry.

Watery Eyes

A sign of conjunctivitis or a cold.

Tumors

Tumors appear as usually yellowish lumps under the skin. Some are cancerous and result in death. Have them examined by a vet.

Overgrown Beaks and Claws

Overgrown beaks are rare and should be treated by a vet. Having a cuttlebone or mineral block in the cage for gnawing diminishes the chances of this occurring.

Overgrown claws are more common, and you can treat them yourself. Trim with dog toenail clippers a little at a time to avoid cutting a blood vessel. If, however, you accidentally happen to nick one bleeding can soon be stopped by using styptic powder and treating with hydrogen peroxide. Smooth any rough edges with a nail file.

Wooden perches help to keep nails trim.

Shock

Usually the result of an injury. The bird stops moving and utters crying sounds, or it may be silent. The eyes do not focus and breathing is shallow.

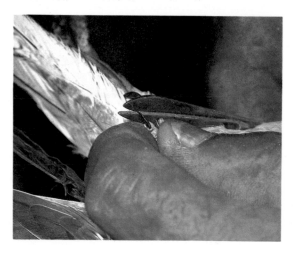

Whatever tool is used, be careful not to cut so much of the claw that bleeding occurs.

This chick has "spraddle leg," which probably stems from a dietary deficiency.

Move the bird to a warm protected spot. You may wrap it in a cloth, but do not make too much of a fuss. Leave the bird to rest. Put food and water within reach. It may take a while for the bird to respond. Meanwhile, check for injury and treat.

Ingrown Feathers
These appear as lumps at the base of a feather follicle which grow larger as the feather grows but can't push out. Have this treated by a vet.

Arthritis and Rheumatism
Often the result of wet perches or perches that are too small in diameter for a proper grip. The best prevention is a variety of perches in various diameters.

Lameness/Sore Feet
Soak foot in warm water or under a light stream of running water for five minutes. Do not get the rest of the bird

Keep in mind that some plants, like the poinsettia, are poisonous, and a Cockatiel should not be allowed access to them.

wet. Dress the foot with iodine or Mercurochrome. Leave uncovered.

Concussion

Symptoms resemble shock. Commonly the result of flying into mirrors, windows, or walls. Administer the same treatment as in shock. Try to make the flying area as safe as possible.

Egg Binding

Egg binding can occur in single females as well as breeding birds. Some females lay eggs regularly even without a mate. The bird will draw on its own calcium if the diet is insufficient to make eggshells. It needs exercise and a good diet.

Keep the bird warm and quiet. If it is tame, apply two or three drops of mineral oil to the vent. Never attempt to push the egg out yourself. If the egg breaks inside of the bird, death is imminent. Call the vet for further advice.

Medicines that come in liquid form may be administered with an eyedropper.

BREEDING

Cockatiels are one of the easiest parrots to breed. The entire breeding cycle from laying eggs to weaning the chicks takes about 2½ months. This can be a time of enjoyment or disappointment. The process may proceed without problems, or breeding may not occur at all. If it becomes necessary for you to hand-rear the chicks, it means a great deal of confinement for you. But the excitement of seeing newborn chicks is enough for most people to take the chance to breed their cockatiels.

Even the tamest birds may be aggressive towards their owners during breeding. Therefore, you may want to keep your original birds as pets and buy others for breeding.

Even though cockatiels may be fertile as young as six months of age, mature adults about a year and a half to two years old are best for breeding. If you feed your pets a regular diet, they will always be in top condition. The same essentials are needed in the diet even without breeding. Changes or supplements are unnecessary. However, if you purchase a bird and are unsure if it has been properly fed, provide an enriched diet for five to six months to be sure it is ready for breeding. Poor nutrition results in egg binding, illness in the breeding pair, and infertile eggs. The parents may refuse or not be able to take proper care of their young.

Include plenty of fresh green vegetables in the diet. Toasted wheat bread, corn, oats and fruits, like strained bananas, should be provided every day, even if the birds do not seem to accept it. Putting a few drops of wheat germ oil on the food is a healthy supplement. Breeding birds also increase their consumption of grit and cuttlebone.

FACING PAGE: A female Cockatiel preens the crest feathers of her mate.

With this diet the birds need lots of exercise to avoid becoming overweight. Confined birds are more difficult to breed, and the exercise decreases the incidence of egg binding, infertile eggs, and stress. Extend the birds' liberties by increasing their free-flying time. If possible, set up a small room, a guest room or heated basement, for the breeding pair. Leave the cage door open for them to come and go as they please.

Household birds are not exposed to great temperature changes. Because of the temperature control in homes and the regularity of a good diet, these birds can be brought into breeding condition at any time. The preferred time is spring, though, when more seeding grasses and vegetables are available. The longer days mean the adults have more light hours to care for the young. Summer is usually too hot and cold weather increases the chances of a bird getting chilled.

Most importantly, be sure the pair you have chosen consists of a male and female. Then, if they are compatible, a

Mate feeding — one element of courtship among Cockatiels.

Breeding

Cockatiels naturally nest in tree cavities.

bond will soon develop. Cockatiels exhibit strong male-female "marital" bonds that will make re-pairing difficult. In the wild, it is not unusual for mates to remain together for life.

Breeding Cages

The breeding cage should be large enough lengthwise for the birds to fly across. Good measurements are 4 x 4 ft. and two to three feet wide, in a location with little interference. Supply enough perches to accommodate two adult birds and about five young.

Nest Boxes

Without a proper nest, breeding will not occur. The birds should have no fear of entering or leaving the nest box. A suitable one can be bought at minimal cost, or you can construct one yourself out of wood or cardboard.

Wood is warmer and can be reused. Cardboard is less expensive, easier to work with, and easily disposed of. Both materials are suitable; it is just a matter of your individual preference. Just be sure the nest box is large enough for two birds and their babies. If it is too small, the adults may step on the eggs and break them. A good size is about 12 × 16 inches by 12 inches high.

Cut a round hole, about two and a half inches in diameter, in the lower corner three inches from the bottom. This is large enough for the birds to pass through and small enough for privacy. Ventilation holes are placed around the sides.

Half of the top needs to be open to give you access to remove the chicks if necessary. Cardboard boxes can be cut and bent back when needed. For wood, use hinges.

Cover the bottom of the box with a sheet of plastic, helpful when it comes time to clean. An inch or two of wood shavings or pine bedding is next. Other soft material can be used, but no cotton or cloth.

In the rear, on the opposite side of the door, attach a nest frame, 1 x 2 or 2 x 2 inches. This prevents the eggs from rolling and keeps the young together for warmth.

The nest box can be placed in the cage or attached outside to provide more room. Use wire clippers to cut 3-4 rungs from the cage. Line up the entrance to the nest box and secure with hooks. The cage can later be patched with wire from a hanger or a piece of metal.

Clean the cage every day and replenish the food. Leave the birds alone for the rest of the time. Continue to provide fresh bath water. Some birds may bathe twice a day now, which helps to keep the eggs moist and prevent binding.

The birds will customize their nest box. Once you notice an increased intake of gravel and cuttlebone, the eggs will soon arrive, about four days after copulation.

Mating and Incubation

Mating is often immediate, but can take up to 4 to 6 weeks. During courtship, the birds are always together and there is much mutual preening. No elaborate displays will be evident. Then the male mounts the female. He uses his claws to gain a foothold on her back. For this reason, a lame male bird is usually no good for breeding.

During incubation, adults deposit their droppings out of the nest. The hen's may be larger, looser, a lighter green than usual and less frequent. There is no cause for concern.

Prior to laying, the female may look ruffled and bloated. Her breathing is more labored and noticeable.

The birds will be in the nest box together when the eggs are laid. The female may labor up to ten hours for each egg, while the male sits on those already laid.

One egg will be laid every other day. The eggs will be

pure white and much smaller than chicken eggs. There can be anywhere from three to nine eggs in a clutch, with the average being about five. It will take from 18 to 20 days for them to hatch. Each is at a different stage of development. They will hatch in the same order in which they were laid, at one- to two-day intervals.

You may notice that the hen sits from dusk to dawn, while the cock sits from dawn to late afternoon. In the afternoon, the mates may spend some time together outside the nest. There may be many times that the couple will sit together on the eggs and chicks.

As is usual with cavity-nesting birds, Cockatiel eggs are white.

Hearing the chicks peep will be your first clue that they have hatched. They are covered with bright yellow down. At one week pin feathers will be evident, starting with the wing, tail and crest.

The parents will grasp the chicks by the beak and vigorously shake their heads up and down. This facilitates the regurgitation method used for feeding. At first, the babies will be fed only a tiny bit. As time passes, they will appear overfed because of the distended crop (a lump at the base of the throat that is now usually full).

A nest box with an entrance hole in the side may be attached on the outside of the cage.

The peeping will get progressively louder, and flapping can be heard inside the nest. The chicks will poke their heads out at around four weeks. They may run and hide at the sight of you. Once they are out of the nest, it is only a few hours before they learn to fly.

At five to six weeks they leave the nest for good. Still fed by their parents, the chicks display an interest in seed and grasses. The weaning process has begun, and they do not return to the nest.

At about eight weeks, the chicks are totally independent and can be removed from the cage. Be sure they are weaned, or they will lose weight and become ill.

The chicks can be placed in new homes at ten weeks. Before you proceed with breeding, it is a good idea to call a local dealer and ask if they will buy the young.

Cleaning the Nest Box

Ideally, the nest box should be cleaned every week after the young are hatched. If the parents react too strongly, do not persist. In their excitement, they may cause harm to the young by trampling them.

Never put your hand in the nest box while the adults are in. Wait until they are out, then block the entrance and remove the box for cleaning. Set the chicks aside in a small container, then replace the soiled contents with fresh shavings.

Cockatiel nestlings: two Lutinos and two Pearls.

(Some people replace the nest box altogether.) Put the chicks back and return the box.

If you plan to use the nest box next season, disinfect it and air it for 24 hours before putting it in the cage for the new breeding.

Hand-rearing the Chicks

This is a full-time job over several weeks or months. Hand-rearing should not be attempted unless the chicks are abandoned, abused or failing to thrive. Cockatiels that are

hand-reared are usually weaker and less desirable. They are more easily trained, though, since they know the one who feeds them as "mother."

The chicks should be kept in an incubator at 95 degrees for about two weeks. A cardboard box with a heating pad underneath it will suffice. Because the chicks have no feathers, they cannot maintain body heat. If the temperature is too high, the birds will pant and appear stressed. Turn down the heat or place a towel between the pad and the box. Keep the lid closed.

Their diet should be pureed and consist of:

crumbled toasted wheat bread
sunflower seed or millet meal
baby peas or green beans
cod liver oil
vitamin supplement
enough warm water to soften this mash but not make it soggy

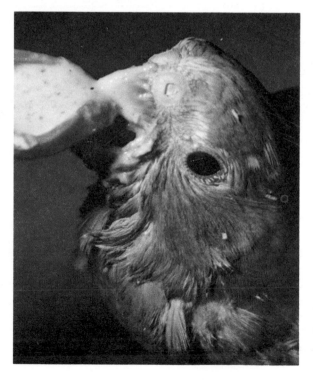

A Cockatiel chick receiving hand-rearing formula from a spoon.

Readily accessible soaked seed encourages a Cockatiel chick to begin eating on its own.

OR

2 c. high protein baby cereal
½ c. wheat germ
¼ c. corn meal
warm water

You may want to wrap the young in a towel to keep them warm. The chicks can be fed from an eye dropper or from a spoon. Keep the crop full; it should never appear empty. After feeding, wipe the chicks clean with a damp cloth or cotton swab. Dried food may be irritating and cause sores. Push out excess air, but do not squeeze the chick.

The babies need to be fed every few hours. A typical schedule to follow is:

1-4 days: every 2-3 hours
5-9 days: every 3-4 hours
10-14 days: every 4-6 hours to be maintained until the end of the feedings. The first feeding is about 6 a.m., the last about 10-11 p.m. It seems likely that the parents do not feed their young throughout the night.

At two to three weeks, provide water in the box. Also, put some of their mixture in a dish and encourage them to eat from it.

Sometime around five weeks, the chicks will attempt to fly. Now they can be moved from the box to a cage. They can even be put in with adults, but watch for abuse and remove them.

Hand-reared chicks are usually dependent longer. Weaning will begin at 7-8 weeks. Feed them in the morning, then leave containers of seed and formula for them during the day. Feed again late evening. Offer green leafy vegetables, and begin to look for cracked seeds in and around the cage. Around 10 weeks, discontinue the hand feedings.

Young Cockatiels in an outdoor flight.

Breeding

Failure To Breed

Possibly a sign of illness, or maybe the birds need a change. It could be a new location or a different type of bedding material. Maybe a new mate is indicated.

No Eggs

If breeding took place but there are no eggs, you need a new hen. If the eggs are clear, showing no vascularity when held to a light, they are infertile. A new male is needed.

Egg Binding

See the disease section.

A Lutino Cockatiel chick at the pin-feather stage.

In Conclusion

No more than two broods per year should be expected, or the pair will become run-down, resulting in infertile eggs or improper care of the young. Remove the breeding nest after one or two clutches, to interrupt the cycle. Be observant and punctual, for it is not uncommon for mating to occur while some chicks are still being weaned.

The following books by T.F.H. Publications are available at pet shops everywhere.

ENCYCLOPEDIA OF COCKATIELS
By George A. Smith
(PS-743)

SUGGESTED READING

After placing the Cockatiel in the context of other parrots and relating the history of its domestication, Dr. Smith discusses it first as a pet: selection, care, taming, and talking. A chapter on behavior in the wild introduces the selection on breeding, which covers accommodations, maintenance, the breeding cycle, and problems that may arise. Comments on each of the color varieties are succeeded by an exposition of the genetics involved. The final chapter deals with health maintenance. "If you needed to limit yourself to one book on cockatiels, this is the volume I would suggest." Arthur Freud in *American Cage-Bird Magazine.*
Illustrated with 60 color and 108 black-and-white photos.
Hard cover, 5½ x 8″, 256 pp.

COCKATIELS, A COMPLETE INTRODUCTION—By Elaine Radford
Hardcover CO-012; Paperback CO-012S
The budgerigar's larger cousin will be introduced to many new bird fanciers through the medium of this fine new book, one that's fun to read as well as being a real eye-opener about how to select and take care of cockatiels.
Contains 99 full-color photos and 8 full-color line drawings. 5½ x 8½, 128 pages.

ALL ABOUT BREEDING COCKATIELS—By Dorothy Bulger (PS-801)

Discusses breeding Cockatiels, artificial incubation and hand-rearing, hand-taming and talking, grooming and health problems, and adds helpful hints.
Illustrated with 30 color and 20 black-and-white photographs.
Hard cover, 5½ x 8", 96 pp.

COCKATIEL HANDBOOK—By Gerald R. Allen and Connie Allen (PS-741)

This authoritative handbook on keeping and breeding Cockatiels is the outgrowth of many years of a study and observation by a husband-and-wife team living in Australia. It covers anatomy, natural history, pet care, and diseases and illness.
Illustrated with 77 color and 96 black-and-white photos.
Hard cover, 5½ x 8½", 256 pp.

Index